Always Bring An Extra Pair of Shoes

Preparing For Leadership

Samuel Wayne West

Always Bring an Extra Pair of Shoes

For more information email samuelwaynewest@gmail.com. Also follow Samuel's YouTube channel, *Samuel Wayne West - What Sam Said.*

Interior and Cover Build by Infinity Flower Publishing, LLC
www.infinityflowerpublishing.com

ISBN 978-1-7361933-2-7 (paperback)

Dedication

This book is dedicated to my parents: the late Sam West, Jr., and Clyde and Bettye Zachery. Thank you for being a great example and your unconditional love. I am a better person because of you.

Acknowledgements

This book is the result of years of journaling, prayer, study, and reflections from my leadership experiences over the last thirty years. To each minister, motivational speaker, past and present supervisors, friends, mentors, and others who I have learned from, I say, thank you. I have listened to hundreds of messages, attended seminars, and read books on a variety of topics in preparation for this body of work. Although I don't recall all of the names, I thank and acknowledge each of you for your contributions.

I am thankful for my wife, Katriece, and resident editor, my daughter, Samaria. I am also grateful for my extended family, who serve as daily reminders of what leadership is, what should be included as part of my story, and what should be dismissed. They were the first to remind me that not everything I chew has to be swallowed. Many of their thoughts and pearls of wisdom have found their way into the story I will share with you.

To Joel Boyce, thank you for sharing your editorial talent with me. You were a Godsend.

Contents

Chapter One

Always Bring an Extra Pair of Shoes

A few years ago, my daughter and I took a day trip to Seattle, Washington. She has always been fascinated with the city and wanted to visit the comic book stores near the wharf. I knew we would be walking a lot, so I told her to make sure she wore comfortable shoes. She had purchased a new pair of tennis shoes and wanted to wear them. I said, "Ok, but bring along another pair just in case." Although it sounds random, I immediately thought back to a field trip I took to Six Flags as an elementary student. My grandmother had purchased me a new pair of sandals, and I was excited to wear them. She said, "Wayne, there will be a lot of walking. You probably should wear your sneakers. I said, "Ok," but in my mind, I thought, *She never has been to Six Flags. How would she know?* I didn't listen. I just had to show off my sandals, so I put them on. She said, "You probably should wear your tennis shoes." I said, "I want to wear my new shoes." She didn't say anything else. She just looked at me and smiled. Off my cousin, Connie, and I went. We had our sack lunch and a few dollars to spend. What a day it was going to be!

When I opened my lunch, there were two neckbone sandwiches with hot sauce and mustard. I quickly placed the sandwiches back into the heavily greased brown paper bag because I was embarrassed. Other students had peanut butter and jelly or ham and cheese sandwiches with potato chips. Connie and I had neckbone sandwiches. Really? Who sends their child on a field trip with a neckbone sandwich? I decided I wasn't hungry. Connie, on the other hand, opened her bag and started to eat without any embarrassment at all, I might add. When one of our classmates asked her if she had another one and wanted to trade lunches, I learned a valuable lesson. What you despise or what makes you feel ashamed is what someone else longs to have. You see, the student hated peanut butter and jelly sandwiches. When I saw what happened, I eagerly said, "I have two. You can have one of mine!"

We arrived in Atlanta and received our instructions for the day. It was the perfect day until it started to rain. It went from a light sprinkle to a heavy downpour that lasted over an hour. It didn't take long for the glue that held the sole of one of my "new" shoes to come apart. It was uncomfortable, and I had to walk very slowly, or the sole would flap behind me. I missed a lot of the rides because once I got there, most of my friends were way ahead of me in the line. I thought of my grandmother's words, "Wayne, wear your tennis shoes, or at least bring them if you need them." By the time I made it back to the bus, I had a sore on my ankle and an obvious limp.

In Seattle, my daughter and I were halfway through our one-day excursion when the back of her right shoe started to rub against her ankle. We had completed our tour of the Space Needle and were heading to the comic book store. She didn't say anything initially, but by the time we left the first store, a small bruise had appeared on the back of her ankle. She had not "tried" or worn the shoes before, and she didn't realize the fit wasn't as comfortable as she thought. I said, "Hey, why don't you put on the other shoes I asked you to pack in your backpack?" She said, "I didn't think I would need them." Subsequently, we purchased a pack of Band-Aids and placed one on the back of her heel. The intent was to at least minimize the bruising, but the moral of the story is when someone who has more experience and knowledge in an area offers a suggestion, you should at least consider it. Just because it sounds like something you think won't work or isn't needed, you still should heed that person's counsel.

Napoleon Hill, author of *Think and Grow Rich*, said, "Those who are afraid of new ideas are doomed before they start." Often, people will hear me say, "Always pack an extra pair of shoes." It's not that the idea on which we agreed won't work, but there always should be a contingency plan. You even should have a contingency plan for the contingency plan. You may not like neckbone sandwiches, but there is always someone waiting for you to offer your gift, your talent, and your resources as a seed for his/her miracle. What we sometimes "hide" is what someone else needs to be his/her seed. You can't reap a harvest on what you need to lead successfully by holding onto the seed you think has no value.

Chapter Two

The Power of Your Voice

An influence is something or someone who impacts our ability to make sound, logical decisions. All of us are influenced by what we read, watch on television, or listen to on the radio. We are influenced by the relationships we have and by the people with whom we connect on social media. Our conversations with family and friends have the potential to sway our position on social, political, and religious viewpoints. We are the sum of all the experiences we have had in our lives including the good, the bad, and the experiences we don't mention. Do you put your ketchup in the refrigerator or leave it in the pantry as your mom did? Do you prefer cold or room temperature water because someone you trust said room temperature is better for you? How we handle our finances, raise our children, drive, and prepare our meals is a result of someone else's influence. It is no different in leadership.

Dr. Henry Cloud, author of *9 Things a Leader Must Do*, shares that, "Leadership success is more tied to a pattern of thinking and moving forward that learns from mistakes and stays focused on goals." It does not say we won't make mistakes. The goal is to learn from the ones we do make. While discussing the topic of personal development, Jim Rohn said we should learn from our experiences, learn from other people's experiences, and learn from observation. My cousin, Sandy, shared a social media post recently that said, "Grow through what you go through." We must learn from our past encounters and use the experiences to become more effective leaders. Before you have that courageous conversation or make a decision that could alter the trajectory of someone's life, you should take into consideration what has influenced your decision-making.

What prior experiences have framed your thoughts? What mentors and former bosses have shaped your leadership style? What are the core guiding principles that dictate your behavior and control how you will respond or will not respond? What did or didn't work in your past that helps you understand the value of knowing when to speak and when to be silent?

John Maxwell said we influence at least ten thousand other people in our lifetime. Therefore, when you look in the mirror, you are not just looking at *yourself*. You are looking at everyone you have encountered throughout your life plus the influence of their character, convictions, and commitment to success that made an imprint on you. I once read a Chinese proverb that said, "The tongue can paint what the eyes can't see." The power that comes from one voice can be enough to make a difference, alter a course of events, and influence personal and professional outcomes. It matters what you say. The right words spoken at the right time without the right emotion still can fall on deaf ears. Friedrich Nietzsche said, "We often refuse to accept an idea merely because the tone of voice in which it has been expressed is unsympathetic to us." The ultimate litmus test to determine if communication has achieved its goal is when the message that is sent is received accurately by whoever hears it.

One of my favorite movie quotes from *Rush Hour* is when Chris Tucker says to Jackie Chan, "Do you understand the words that are coming out of my mouth?" How many of us leaders have been there? Try as we may, we still end up with a disconnect between the expectations we shared and the sometimes brutal reality of the outcomes we receive. "I didn't understand what you said. Did you give it to me in writing?" That one statement over a decade ago taught me the value of communicating orally and in writing. You always can go back to the email, signed acknowledgement form, or what I like to call a memorandum of understanding signed by all parties to find common ground for discussion and move forward. It is funny when they look at the document and say, "Oh, yes. I remember now."

Dr. Myles Munroe said, "Being able to stand before people and they listen to you is a dangerous privilege." We cannot take lightly the power we hold as a leader, regardless of our level in the organization. Our voice sets the course for either success or failure in the lives of those entrusted to us. As a leader, I often find myself asking, *Does my voice match my value?* In some instances, I think, *Does my voice void my value? Did what I share help or harm an already fragile situation?* I was talking with a friend a few weeks ago when about halfway through the conversation, I asked, "How does what you say add value to what we are discussing?" He paused and said, "I don't know." I was reminded of how much time we spend talking with people who do not add worth or value to the "whom" we are striving to become.

Being a leader means understanding that there are 24 hours in a day. Those same 24 hours that one man can use to change the direction of his life are the same 24 hours another man can use to change the direction of his life. One change may be for his good, and the other change may be for his detriment. If I choose to spend some of that time with you, we both should benefit from our encounter. I am thankful for the lessons I have learned. Life and experiences (others and our own) can frame our perspective. Be careful not to look at people and judge the worth of their character based on the decisions they made because they had no other choice. You don't know what forces were at play, and you don't know what you would have done if you were in their position. I spoke with someone recently who said, "After 58 years, I am finally able to look in the mirror and be happy with the person looking back at me." He told me that when he was a young boy in elementary school, his dad would tell him, "You never will amount to anything. Stop saying that you want to go to college." After hearing it for so long, he began to believe it. It wasn't until he was in high school that a teacher saw in him what his father failed to see or acknowledge. He was accepted into college, and he graduated. Now, he serves as a manager in a financial company. When I asked him what made him the proudest, he said, "Being able to speak life into my daughter and see in her what I always knew was in me." We never will understand why people choose to do some of the things they do. Someone asked me, "Why did you do that?" I said, "My response revolved around my circumstances at that time. I am not the same person now." I recognize my worth and the impact the words coming from my mouth have on my life. In the end, I will have to give an account for my words and actions, not yours.

In *Letters to a Young Sister*, former First Lady Michelle Obama said, "Own who you are." I believe one of the steps to harness the power of your voice is to own and accept who you are - yes, all of you. This process will require you to evict the negative words, deeds, and actions of others and mentally move out of the "you" their words created. Just because people can speak TO you does not give them the privilege to speak INTO you. Your heart does not know the difference. It is designed to give a harvest to the words that are planted. Be mindful of what you see. Be mindful of what you hear and be mindful of what you say. I am reminded of what Uncle Ben shared with Spider-Man when he said, "With great power comes great responsibility." Developing the power of your voice will take time. It may start as a whisper like a young Simba but keep roaring. There is a Mufasa hidden in all of us.

Chapter Three

Many

Many leaders have learned that you should not commit to what you can't do once you get put in the game. You are not ready yet. There is a time when the call to leadership will come. Until then, there is a season to learn from the bench. Stop pouting and start shouting for the team! In a championship game, all the players get a ring.

Many aspiring leaders want the promotion, but they don't want the pruning that proceeds it. Just because a seat at the table is available does not mean it belongs to you. Learn how to sow where you are now, so you can reap at YOUR appointed time. The worst seat at the table is the one not destined for you.

Many want the crown, but they don't want the cross that goes along with it. Many want the title and have the correct knowledge, but they lack wisdom. They do not know how and when to use their knowledge. Just because you can doesn't always mean you should. Many want to lead but have not yielded to being led.

Many things leaders do may never be seen or heard. Learn to applaud and encourage yourself even if you have to do it alone.

Many times, I walked in the rain. Sometimes, I walked for pleasure. Sometimes, I walked so no one would know I was crying. I am glad they could not tell the difference between my tears and the wetness of the rain.

Many come to realize you won't know where your "leaks" are in your ability to lead in a storm until it rains. We need the rain. It washes away things that show us the depth of who we are and what we truly have. Many know that as you grow, your coverage grows. There may come a time when you cannot share your umbrella with the people after the storm whom you shared it with during the storm.

Many have learned that just because you make it look easy to others doesn't mean that it was or is easy. When your natural gifts work in tandem with His grace, that is where you will find true success. It is not you, but rather, it is His favor that is upon you.

Many have lied, stolen, cheated, and manipulated to get a job only to find themselves having to lie, steal, cheat, and manipulate to keep the job. Many have learned that just because someone was a great employee does not mean he/she will be a great supervisor. Make sure you choose wisely when you have the privilege to appoint.

Many realize it is a waste of time building the perfect team; it doesn't exist because we are not perfect people. Focus on creating the RIGHT and the most effective team in which individuals' abilities match the need, goal, or task.

Many have learned that you can't see what you aren't looking at. There is power in being visible. Some refer to it as management by wandering. Get up. Walk. Talk. Ask. Many have learned that success is a team effort. Choose your teammates wisely. If you want to win, choose winners.

Many have learned there is always a way forward, even if it requires a step back first. It is your job as a leader to figure it out. Many have grown weary IN the work, but the key is not to become weary OF the work.

Chapter Four

Build a Better You

A lot of research speaks to skills, beliefs, and values essential to charter the path to leadership successfully. These character traits, principles, and core values apply to multiple fields, particularly in times of crisis. In the *Power of Now*, Eckhart Tolle said, "Accept – then act. Whatever the present moment presents, accept it as if you had chosen it. Always work with it, not against it. Make it your friend and ally, not your enemy." During phases of personal and professional transformation, one has to hold near the core values of faith, trust, and hope, looking forward with reasonable confidence that this too shall pass. When it appears bleak, and sometimes it will, I often refer back to what CEO and Superintendent, Dr. Morcease J. Beasley, once shared with a group of district and school leaders. He said, "Sometimes, you have to steal the faith of others when you don't have the strength to see it on your own." There are many areas of success in which I look back and see it wasn't one particular task that brought home the trophy. There were many instances when I had to trust what had been shared with me until I could believe for myself. Always remember to celebrate the small wins along the way. I remember a radio minister once said, "As you move in faith, take it one step at a time, and each step will be a miracle."

Every Day is Now

I walked into an emergency room a few years ago. After waiting to be seen by a doctor, I eventually was escorted to the triage area. One of the first things the health care practitioner did was to check my blood pressure and ask me a series of questions. I guess it didn't matter whether I had a broken collarbone or a headache. The initial wait was part of the process. What followed was another period of waiting before I was able to be seen by a physician. He shared that he reviews the data from the initial screening, so it can be used as a baseline to determine when a patient is healthy or not. Then, he asks questions to make determinations from there regarding care or treatment. He shared that they may have to ask additional questions about family history, etc. I immediately thought of what one of my doctor friends said to me while he was in medical school. He said, "We are in the practice of medicine. We ask questions, so we can prescribe the best treatment possible."

Ask yourself, *When was the last time I checked my area, department, school, or business's vital signs before I shared a new assignment or project?* As we prepare to lead, now more than ever, we have to do a pulse check. We need to be as intentional as an emergency room doctor by confirming we have the correct data to make the decision before prescribing treatment. We have to look at WHY we are here and WHAT are the needs we need to meet. I remember the conversations we had in our district regarding system redesign. I remember the facilitator shared, "The goal is not to force people to change. Our goal is to get stakeholders to look at what we have in place, the what is - the NOW – and then be courageous in taking proactive steps toward potential possibilities of what we envision WILL BE." Recognize that every day is NOW. Yesterday was NOW when it was yesterday. Tomorrow will be NOW when it comes.

Dr. Samuel Chand, the author of *Bigger, Faster Leadership*, shared that we cannot evaluate people and their roles without analyzing what is already in place. Do you have gifted, competent, and dedicated people who fail because the current system doesn't draw out their best? Have you considered that the person who led prior to the pandemic may not be the best candidate to lead in this phase of organizational chaos. Does that person have the necessary technical skills as we pivot from one method of learning to another?

Is that the right person to shift from one method of conducting business to one that now heavily depends on technology in order to make a profit?

As a leader, decisions are not always black and white. Leading and managing through change will show you there is always some gray as you become face-to-face with your defining moment. What worked yesterday may not work today. As you reflect, what do you believe about your impact or your ability to lead during uncomfortable times? Trust me. There is value in learning the art of knowing when to hold them or fold them in the midst of leading.

Lace Up!

During a ministry retreat for pastors and leaders, Pastor Theo McNair, Jr. reminded us of the difference between growth and development. Growth, for the most part, is automatic. Development takes an intentional, focused effort. To build a better leader, YOU have to build a better YOU. Early in my career, someone suggested I get a mentor. I needed to find someone preferably in the profession I had chosen. I needed to find someone further along than I, and I needed someone from whom I could receive advice and counsel. I needed to find someone who was not afraid to tell me what I needed to hear, even if it was not what I wanted to hear. Mentors are in our lives to help, lead, guide, and point us in the direction that hopefully will advance our careers. I also found out that you can have more than one mentor.

As you grow, your personal and professional needs change. My first mentor was just who I needed when I graduated from college. When I got my personal feelings and my pride out of the way, I was able to see the things that he shared with me were for my good. My second mentor helped fine-tune my communication skills, and he told me that just because you are a great speaker does not mean people will want to hear what you have to say. He also told me that I shouldn't take it personally if a particular audience didn't have an ear to hear what I said. My third mentor taught me that I must learn the nuances of the industry and work on the things that matter. Not everything matters, and not everyone values your time. I was able to receive something from each mentor and still glean from them to this day. Are you surrounded by people who hold you accountable and propel you to change or are you surrounded by people who have allowed you to stay the same? Are you surrounded by those who prefer not to hurt your feelings to keep your friendship? Ask yourself after an encounter with them, *What leadership "residue" did they leave behind or was it just sweat?*

John Maxwell said, "One of the keys to successful leadership is applying the concepts that have made other leaders strong." To become an effective leader, you have to go through the process. During this period of waiting, learn to work on yourself. What are those personal characteristics and traits that will set you apart from others who are climbing the same ladder? What are those character flaws and traits that could be the hindrance to your advancement? Both are important to know. Sometimes, we get so caught up with what we feel is wrong with our leaders and what others have said that we don't take the time to see all the "right" in them. There is a reason they lead the way they lead. The only thing that gives you experience is experience. Minister Mike Owens said, "I can't slow down as a leader until you catch up." A colleague of mine once said, "I wouldn't do that if I was you." I responded, "You are not me." For me to achieve my goal and run the race that has been laid out for me, I need people who are ready, willing, and able to run! It is hard to prepare for the race when you have no laces in your shoes.

As a Man or Woman Thinks

When you are building a better you or an equally important better team, you have to focus on selecting talent who will add value. Don't sleep on the recruitment and retention processes. When you are seeking highly qualified applicants, you need to be able to see the "who" they present as well as the "who" they have the potential of becoming. Both are important. If not, we end up with someone who is hireable, but the person is not promotable. A wise person said, "Your life is always moving in the direction of your strongest thoughts." How you think ultimately will determine how you lead. The people with whom you think will determine whether you leap or limp. Who are your thought partners? We all need them.

Have you ever had a thought that you knew had the potential to build your leadership capacity, blow your sales quota out of the roof, or jump-start your entrepreneurial enterprise, but you did not write it down? Have you ever listened to a podcast that was just what the doctor ordered, and you wanted to share the motivational message with your team, but you got distracted and didn't get the name or "screenshot" the title, and when you searched for it, you couldn't find it? How many thoughts have we had that we did not write down that "left" us? I recall a message I heard on a radio broadcast during which the minister said, "You have to strike while it's hot." Those creative ideas and those witty inventions that come to us have a lifespan. Leonard Ravenhill said, "The opportunity of a lifetime must be seized in the lifetime of that opportunity." Pay close attention. He said it must be done in the lifetime of **that** opportunity, not **an** opportunity. Meaning, you just can't jump at everything that passes your way. My Aunt Barbara said, "Everybody talking about it is what it is. I say, 'It ain't what it ain't.'" Know the difference.

Sometimes, we learn our greatest lessons in the middle of a storm. Under whose umbrella are you standing during the storm? Does it have holes in it? What lessons do you find yourself repeating again and again because you did not learn from them the first time? Is it always 'someone else?' Should you have stayed where you were and submitted yourself to your prior boss or supervisor before you took another assignment? Ammishaddai Grand-Jean, author of *Benchwarmer*, shared that life is all about timing. He went on to say, "We often miss lessons and blessings because we move in haste and forget there are things to learn before we can levitate." Have you not learned that those with authority are under authority? He didn't give you the answer you wanted, so you quit. Is there a crack in your character that you refuse to address that keeps you running like a hamster on a wheel? You are tired. You are diligently moving but going nowhere fast. Here is the biggie. Did you find out that it wasn't them? It was you. To get the influence, favor, and the mantle of your leader, you have to stay close.

My Uncle Bill shared with me early in my leadership journey that there always will be issues. He said that as the leader, it is my responsibility to offer a solution. Pastor Theo McNair, Jr. shared that how well you do in life depends not only on what you do, but whom you do it with. In order to build a better you, you have to look at those with whom you are connected. Not everyone who can speak into your life has earned the right to do that. Be intentional about how you are connected to them. If you hear something long enough, you will start to believe it. If those with whom you workout in the "gym" of your personal development are not aligned with your values and expectations, it's time to change your membership.

Chapter Five

You Can't Please Everybody

W: The Silent Letter in leadership

W: Who are you following?

W: Who are you studying?

W: What books are you reading"

W: What webinars have you participated in?

W: What personal self-care habits have you adopted?

W: What does your presence "speak?" Are you just present (physically, but you bring no intellectual capital with you)?

W: Why should they hire you?

W: When you walk into a room, do you bring all of YOU with you?

W: What are you worth?

W: What do you need to do to be socially and emotionally healthy? A broken leader cannot teach another broken leader how to be whole.

W: When you realize very few things grow in dry places, you will understand the importance of hydration.

W: Winning. Until you taste it, it will be easy to quit.

W: What do you need to do to be the leader your gift demands?

W: What attributes are you grounded in that make you a great leader?

W: What are the influences that govern how you lead and what are the ones you need to replace or enhance?

W: When you realize that just because you know the company product or content does not mean you know how to talk to people, you will understand that you may need to work on your communication skills. In case you haven't noticed, people don't like you.

W: When you realize that just because you work well with others, does not mean you can lead others - well.

W: Well, I have my own way of doing things.

W: Well, how has that worked out for you?

DOES IT MATTER?

Some things are distractions. They don't matter at the moment, and in some instances, they do not matter at all. Some phone calls are designed to steal your time. Some conversations are not worth having. Some relationships of yesterday are not what we need in the 'season of leadership' that we are in today. They may have added value at one time, but they are a hindrance to our growth now. Some habits and social outings were good for you yesterday, but they add no value to the YOU that you are destined to become tomorrow. Dr. Henry Cloud, author of *9 Things a Leader Must Do*, shared, "Even good things that consume time, resources, energy, and attention and do not get you where you want to go are a negative." What are the "time consumers" you have tolerated that drain you of your ability to lead effectively? What little foxes are spoiling your vine? What (or who) do you need to remove or replace in your life that has caused you to become discouraged and unable to move from where you are? What happened to that spark you had? You were on fire! However, wrong associations have dampened your spirit and your drive.

No matter how hard you try, you cannot burn when you are wet.

Heap See. Few Know

When I was asked what one word would best describe who I am and how I lead, I chose "edutainer." In my personal and professional life, I am an edutainer. It is what I enjoy and what I do. Edutainment has been defined as presenting information through a medium that both entertains and educates; a medium that once engaged and married to your personality, your skills, talents, and your gift will result in *your* message being heard.

From my childhood until now, I have enjoyed seeing people smile and making them laugh. I believe that we all need a good laugh now and then. It helps create a better work environment and lowers people's blood pressure! None of us are perfect. There are things about all of us that we wish were different. I am not you. You are not me, but we each have a message and a story to tell. What works for you may not work for me, and what works for me may not work for you. The purpose or intent of our message may be the same, but it is our presentation that sets us apart.

You may see a cup half empty, but I may see it as a cup that is half full. I may prefer dress slacks and a pair of loafers, and your comfort may lie in jeans and tennis shoes. I prefer reading a good book and watching *Star Trek*. You may prefer taking a walk or watching sports. I am me. You are you. My audience may not be your audience. The challenges I face may not be the ones with which you have to contend. I can't laugh at you because it may be my experience tomorrow.

As a leader, I serve based on the belief that what I do and what I say makes a difference. Who I am on the inside speaks more loudly than who I present on the outside. It does not take people long to determine if what you profess aligns with what you possess. I work daily to model for my team how leadership looks and what leadership does. I shared with my staff that one of my goals is to raise the standard for those who will sit in my seat after me. Every day gives me an opportunity to be better and to learn from my experiences the previous day.

Before I was their leader, I led from where I was. As a teacher, I led. As a department chair, I led. As an assistant principal, I led. As a principal, I lead. When I look for potential leaders, I look for their fruit. We all have interviewed the woulda, coulda, shoulda's. We have interviewed the ones who say all the right things, but they show no evidence. What have they done that has improved or made the organization better from where they are now? While sitting on the bench, do they consistently come to practice? Do they support the "team" from where they are? Are they watching the game, drinking up the Gatorade, or taking selfies? As Ammishaddai Grand-Jean puts it, "One must always be prepared because he never knows when his defining moment will come."

Learn to lead from where you are because there is always someone watching you. Do you walk past a piece of paper on the floor hoping someone else will come and pick it up? If there is a bag of trash outside a teacher's classroom, do you walk past it and call for someone to come get it or do you take it to the dumpster? If the cafeteria is short staffed, do you grab a pair of gloves and help clean tables? If your secretary is out, do you type the urgent memo, or do you wait for him/her to get back in three days? A leader leads by example. Of course, we may not be able to do these tasks every day or be a skilled typist. However, when your staff sees that you are willing to jump in and no job is too small or big for you, it makes them appreciate you as their leader. Although many of them (not all, lol) will say, "Mr. West, you don't have to do that. We got it." For me, there is a deeper meaning.

Every Day is a Great Day at BBCA

I remember my first leadership experience in the academic setting. I was an administrator at a Christian school. We did not have a cafeteria, so we would convert our before and after school room/ Saturday morning faith class/Sunday morning classroom into a cafeteria and serve a catered lunch daily. Our administrative staff had to assist in setting up, helping serve if needed, and assisting in taking the trash out when lunch was over. If we ran out of chicken nuggets, I had to make the "chicken run" to pick up some more! We did not have a full- time custodian, so there were times I had to clean the restrooms and classrooms at the end of the day. Did I always want to do that? No. However, I refused to let it show. My Aunt Lois shared with me, "Your record can take you where your mouth cannot." What people see as something they don't have to do today reminds me of yesterdays when there was no choice but to do them. A lot of people see where you are now. Few know and can appreciate your journey. Our school's theme song had as its main verse, "Every day is a great day at BBCA." Every day may not have started out great, but we had faith and confidence that every day would end up being great, and it did.

It doesn't matter where on the organization flow chart your leadership position falls. It does not matter if the industry is education, business, hospitality, or finance. It does not matter if you run your own company. Inherent in the core of leadership is the fact that sooner or later, you will have to tackle an issue or problem that may be hindering the organization's ability to meet a particular goal. As a leader, what frames your thinking will influence your actions. We must work to make sure that our ineffectiveness is not what is hindering organizational growth. In the *Law of the Lid*, John

Maxwell shares that leadership ability is the lid that determines a person's level of effectiveness. If your leadership rate is only a 6, the level of your effectiveness will be no higher than a 5. We have 24 hours a day. What percentage of your day do you spend building a better you? Be yourself but strive to become a better you.

YOU CAN'T PLEASE EVERYBODY

In former President Theodore Roosevelt's *Man in the Arena* speech, he said:

It is not the critic who counts; not the man who points out how the strong man stumbles, or where the doer of deeds could have done them better. The credit belongs to the man who is actually in the arena, whose face is marred by dust and sweat and blood; who strives valiantly; who errs, who comes short again and again, because there is no effort without error and shortcoming; but who does actually strive to do the deeds; who knows great enthusiasms, the great devotions; who spends himself in a worthy cause; who at the best knows in the end the triumph of high achievement, and who at the worst, if he fails, at least fails while daring greatly, so that his place shall never be with those cold and timid souls who neither know victory nor defeat.

When I embarked upon this leadership journey over thirty years ago, I quickly found myself immersed in how to strike a balance among what people said I should do, how I should do it, and how I should make sure that I didn't disappoint those same people when I did whatever they said I should do, and it did not work out like they said it should. While I was new on the team, I was not new to the game. Like any other aspiring leader, I wanted to make a good impression and "please the people" who trusted that I could do the job.

Life had taught me that on-the-job training only came from being on the job. I knew that experience in an area only comes from having experience in the area. However, once I realized that because

I had minimal exposure in that specific area, and I didn't have the knowledge or background necessary to make an effective decision. I had to seek help. That didn't make me feel any better. Have you ever had an ethical dilemma you had to face? Maybe it was not anything serious or a chargeable offense, but you had to contemplate a course of action with which you disagreed because it did not align with your personal beliefs or work ethic? Have you ever had people make you feel "less than" because you didn't agree with the majority or take a particular side? Have you discovered that right is right? I recall Dr. Douglas Hendrix, Area Superintendent, saying, "I would rather be standing on the side of truth even if I am standing alone."

For some, maybe you have been in a situation in which someone took advantage of your lack of knowledge (not ability) or your eagerness to serve. People will get close to you. They will befriend you. You think they are giving you a pat on the back when in actuality, they are looking for a weak spot to stab you in your back. Jimmie L. Lucas, author of *Custom-Built By God*, shared, "Listen to many, but only hear a few." Not everyone who has your ear has your heart.

What Sam Said

It was no different when I started my "What Sam Said" podcast and began airing the messages on social media. I was already nervous and had to cast down thoughts of people not accepting my "brand." Although I hadn't decided exactly what that brand was going to be or how it would look, I knew it was time for me to move. Pastor Theo McNair, Jr. said, "God will give you more on the way. You have to move first." How many of you have realized that not moving can determine an outcome just as if you had moved? We wait for the perfect season to sow only to realize we have to be as faithful in the dark (when you may not have all the answers) as we are in the light (when things appear to be going well). Therefore, I moved. Instead of raging reviews and "attaboys," I received, "Your message is too long." "Your message is too short." "The books on your bookshelf are a distraction." "Why do you have the same color books on the same shelf? Whose idea was that? "Has anyone told you that your lighting is off? I am sure they have." "Why don't you use a green screen? It will eliminate some of the clutter behind you." "Have you considered using a teleprompter? It is obvious that you are reading from a script, and it is throwing me off." "Why did you select that color for your t-shirt?" "Did you know your hair was thinning? That light shining on your head makes it obvious." "Why do you smack your lips when you speak? I noticed you did it at least six times in your last message." "Do you realize you have a gap? I noticed a couple of your sisters have one too." In my mind, I thought, *Do you have any comments about the message?*

What I'm saying to you as you prepare for leadership or work to enlarge your territory is that folks always will have something to say about you, and they will offer advice on what they think you need to do. During one meeting, I was reminded of what my Uncle Charles said to me. "Be mindful of people who talk loud and say nothing." They will support you on Monday, and by Thursday, they may be your biggest critics. The balance comes in knowing you are doing what YOU have been called to do. Fish swim. Dogs bark. Birds fly. Liars lie, and leaders lead. A colleague of mine shared the lyrics of one of their favorite songs with me when I started my journey as an author. The part that resonated with me was "deliver me from people." I recently read a post on social media that said, "Be mindful when you sit down at a table, and other people are the topic of conversation. When you get up, you will be next."

Chapter Six

Who is Your Andrew?

Who's Your Andrew?

During my second year in Bible school, there was a message delivered on the power of an Andrew in our lives. Every leader needs someone who can operationalize his/her vision. Someone who can provide the legs to thrust your plan forward. Someone who can hear what you don't say as loud as what you do say. Someone who is "ok" with his/her assigned role. Someone who is an asset, not a liability. Someone who is just as happy being behind the camera as those who stand in front of it. Someone groomed to serve with you before he/she even knew you. The Bible speaks of such a person. Andrew was one of John the Baptist's disciples. After he heard Jesus speak, he went and followed Him. Andrew went and told his brother, Simon Peter, about Jesus and brought him to meet the Master. We all need an Andrew on our team. Our Andrew should have an eye for potential talent and help us retain key staff through relationship building. Andrew is the one you may not hear a lot about, but that person is there when it's time for you to execute.

One of his disciples, Andrew, Simon Peter's brother, saith unto Him, there is a lad here, which hath five loves, and two small fishes: but what are they among so many? (John 6:8-9).

The other team members (Disciples) were there, but it was Andrew who spoke. Who is your Andrew? They may not lead praise and worship, but they are the glue that holds the praise team together. They may not be the teacher of the year, but they are the ones who mentor the teachers of the year. They may not be the shift managers, but they are the ones who get there early, check the inventory, and resolve customer issues before they even get to you, and they are the ones people know by name.

They may not be the custodians, but they pick up every piece of paper they see in the hallway. They are the pleasant voice on the main office phone who can settle upset customers on the other line and get them to become repeat customers. They are the employees with the high school degrees from an academic standpoint but have a PhD in life experience and understand that "if two shall touch and agree on anything that they ask, it shall be done." They are your thought partners when you need to run an idea by others. They stand in agreement with you and support you with their voice and their actions. Do you know who your Andrew is?

Do you gravitate towards people based on their outward appearance and not the condition of their heart? You often hear leaders say, "Get people who are like-minded to be on your team." I also will add, "Get someone who is like-spirited with you!" Every person who is with you is not for you. I am sure many of you have found that out already. We assign people tasks because they are faithful, but they may not be the most qualified people to complete the tasks. We place people in the right position but at the wrong time and for the wrong purpose. They needed to develop where they were before we uprooted them. Then, when they are unsuccessful, we try to hold them accountable for something they had neither the desire, talent, skill, or ability to perform. In many instances, it is best to leave them where they are fruitful. I recently heard someone say "There are times when a well-placed pawn is more powerful than a king."

We offer positions to people based on a referral from a friend or colleague. They are not what we need, but we feel that having someone is better than having no one at all, or so we think. The truth is that having the wrong someone is worse than having no one at all. Shortly after they start, we see our mistakes. We understand why these people were looking for a job when we met them. It can take you four weeks to hire someone and three years to write him/her out. A favor has now become a failure.

Lustful Leadership

One of the tidbits that Gayle D. Beebe, in her book, *The Shaping of an Effective Leader*, referenced was lust versus fidelity. Lust, in this context, refers to leaders who think that people exist only to satisfy their desires. Have you experienced managers or leaders who make decisions in their best interest but not in the best interests of the team or the organization? It is what they want, period. I didn't consult you because I don't value you. I am the boss. This position is my ticket to the next level. I don't plan to take you with me, so no matter the cost, do it my way. Sadly, they continue this approach of leading to the detriment of everyone else. I like to refer to it as leadership lust, which, in its simplest form, is an insatiable quest that never will be satisfied. Lustful tendencies in leadership always will want more and another position. As it continues to feed off those entrusted to our care, it eventually erodes the people's confidence in our ability to lead them effectively.

Understand the purpose of those you have been called to lead. Andrews have a purpose. How many relationships end because people want you to be something to and for them that you are not equipped to be? However, because you were present, they ran to you. If you cannot produce fruit at that time, they run to someone else and leave you feeling that you never will meet a need in the organization. It just wasn't my time yet. I didn't have the exposure that would have led me to the experience to expedite your request. I am your Andrew. I am still growing. Don't pluck me up by the root and plant me somewhere I am not destined to grow. Don't discount me to satisfy your lust for power. I may not be what you want, but I am what you need.

When I was preparing for a "What Sam Said" message, I came across an article during a Google search that shed light on why some fig trees we encounter in our lives are barren. The most common reason for a fig tree not producing fruit may be its age. If the fig tree is not old enough to produce seeds, it is unable to produce fruit. It went on to say that a fig tree will not produce fruit until it reaches two years old, but it can take up to six years to reach maturity. Don't allow someone else to come to you prematurely and decide your destiny!

It is not your time yet.

Keep being faithful. Keep sowing positive seeds. Your season of fruitfulness is on its way!

Stay in your Lane.

John Maxwell said, "Good things happen to a team when a player takes the place where he or she adds the most value; when all of the players on the team take the role that maximizes their strengths – their talent, skill, and experience." That's the power of the law of the niche.

Let me ask you a question. Why do we look forward to Aunt Bernice making the sweet potato pies for every family gathering? Is it because they are absolutely delicious, and no one makes a better pie?! Well, Yes! Everyone, well almost everyone, has a favorite dish that he/she contributes to the whole. My mom makes an amazing pot of butter beans and the best hoe cake cornbread this side of the Mississippi. My sister, Nikki's squash casserole and meatballs are always a family favorite. My wife makes a mean meatloaf. My cousin Casey's ribs are a hit. My Aunt Dot's baked turkey wings were always a welcomed treat. My daughters' macaroni and cheese is simply the best, and my cousin Connie's collard greens are always a hit! We can all be in the kitchen and be confident and competent in the dishes we are preparing while we enjoy each other's company. It is nice when people know their role and accept their part in the plan, and there is no spirit of competition among us. What am I saying? Having the right people in the right place with the right skill set is key. It is the basis of what creates an amazing meal that all can enjoy.

Just in case you didn't know, there are two amazing cooks on my administrative team. I mean, they are professional grade! During our first year of virtual learning, we wanted to do something special for our staff. We decided to prepare a meal for Thanksgiving and let everyone drive-through and pick up a plate. It would give us an opportunity to see each other and wave and give well wishes for the holiday break. We met, decided who would prepare what dishes, and assigned roles to ensure that we would stay within the COVID-19 protocols that had been instituted. On the day of the event, we had picture perfect weather, and everything was going smoothly! I was happy that we were able to give back to a group of educators who had given so much to our community. It was going fine until one of us who shall remain nameless decided he would help move things along. About halfway through the drive-in event, we had an outpouring of cars in the lane. It was like everybody got hungry at the same time, so the nameless person thought he would just go behind the serving table and help "speed things along." The containers were pre-fixed, so I thought (I mean, the nameless person). What harm could I cause?

The plates were pre-fixed, so all I had to do was ask what dessert and drink they wanted and hand it to them through the window. Simple enough. Right? I saw a window, and I made my move! I was able to serve about six staff members before one of the assistant principals came from the kitchen and inquired about the plates that had been set aside for those who had selected vegetarian as their option. I said, "Oh, we had some set aside for vegetarians?" I thought they were all the same, so I just grabbed them and gave them out to speed up the line. My assistant principal smiled and said, "We all had our roles. We asked you to stand by the entrance and wave to the staff and thank them for all that they have done. They were looking forward to seeing you. We would be responsible for the meal distribution piece. You had one assignment."

I didn't realize that there was a system in place. I just thought, *How hard can it be to grab a plate and hand it through a window?* Well, what I ended up doing was giving out the vegetarian plates to those five people I served. They wanted chicken. I was then kindly asked to, "Go back and do what you are good at. Let us handle what we are good at." Subsequently, they sent me back to the entrance to wave/smile, thank the staff for the service they had provided to our learning community, and thank them for coming." That taught me firsthand that just because you don't know how something works doesn't mean you are needed to fix it. Stay in your lane and trust your team. Trust the process that has been agreed upon.

Just because you are the team leader, just because you are the "man of the house," and just because you happen to make the most money in your relationship does not mean that you are always right and that you have the answer to every situation that arises. Stay in your lane.

In this business of life, we are not assembling car parts in an automotive plant where they are exactly the same and are attached exactly the same way each time. People with whom we work and live have unique and specific gifts, talents, and abilities. Because they don't do it the way you think is right doesn't mean it is not the right way for that specific task. What am I saying? Just go back out to the curb and wave!

What's Lacking in Your Packing?

While participating in a district leadership class, Deputy Superintendent Dr. Ralph Simpson asked the aspiring principals, "What is lacking in your packing?" I told him that I was going to steal this! As I listened to what he shared, it caused me to pause and look in my "Felix the Cat" bag of tricks to see if I had the tools needed to meet the ever-increasing demands of leadership. As I listened to Dr. Simpson, I thought of the core tenets of what John Maxwell refers to as a "360° leader." They are leaders who work on developing their influence to lead from anywhere in the organization and work on becoming better leaders today than they were yesterday. They model the behavior they desire to see in others and are willing to hire people who are better than themselves. They are the ones who confidently and competently can speak to areas that you cannot address. Jordan Peterson said, "Compare yourself to whom you were yesterday, not to who someone else is today." You don't know everything, and you don't have to know it all. Anyone can turn lemons into lemonade, but as Dr. Shonda Moody Shaw said to me when I was her assistant principal, "West, it is easy to turn lemons into lemonade. All it takes is water and sugar. The question is can you turn lemons into grape juice? That is the mark of leadership."

When I was asked recently what best describes my leadership style, I said situational-ish. I added the "ish" because time and experiences dealing with people have taught me that it is ok to pause and say, "Let me think on that, and I will get back with you," and you feel ok with it as a leader. We don't always know the intentions behind what we are being asked. Mrs. Anna McNair, the co-founder of Believers' Bible Christian Church, said to me in my early years of leadership, "We don't always know the heart of people or their intentions, and we shouldn't assume that we do." We won't always have an answer at the moment the problem or opportunity presents itself. You have to know within yourself that with the right time, the right people, the right professional self-development, and the right environment, the answer will come.

There were times I buckled under the pressure of the people and their voices that spoke loudly in my head, saying, *Why don't you have the answer? Why did they hire you anyway? You don't have the experience. Someone else would have been a better choice for the position. I wonder who he knows.*

It is during these times that your belief in yourself has to be stronger than the belief of those who are against you. Is it easy? Uh, no! However, learn what you need to become a better you. Learn those areas in your "toolkit" that you need to enhance or that may be missing. Check out your leadership suitcase. What is missing? You may not need it today, but as one minister said, "Put it in the freezer, so you can thaw it out when you need it." Make a list just like you do when you pack for a trip. As a leader, what have you forgotten to pack? What keeps coming up that you cannot answer?

As I shared earlier, I started my career in academia in the private school setting. I was a daycare director and school administrator for a Christian K-8th grade academy before transitioning into a public school setting. I spent five years as a teacher and three years as an assistant principal at a charter school before I received my assignment as a principal. Each step along the way and every progression provided exposure for me on various levels and allowed me to see parts of my character that needed to change. Through it all, including disappointments, joy, successes, and failures, I began to see the heart of the quote by William Johnsen that says, "If it is to be, it is up to me." I learned that what I believe, what I say, and what I accept about myself will determine the path my life will take. I speak that over myself to make the difference. It is my words, not your words, that will bear fruit in my life.

We all have had someone say or do something we did not like, and those words may have left a scar. We must let it go before it begins to eat us from the inside. Continuing to pick at the scab only will delay healing. As author Jeremy Shorter shared in *Your Guide to a Sound Mind*, "Forgiveness is the healing process for you to move forward." Anne Lamott put it this way, "Not forgiving is like drinking rat poison and then waiting for the rat to die." In this instance, it is not about them or what they said or did. It is about you and your well-being.

WHY DON'T YOU KNOW?

I recall one parent during an Open House meeting asking me a question during my first year as a public school principal. It was my third day on the job. I responded to her question, "I am not sure, but I can get back with you? May I have your contact information, so I can follow up with you tomorrow?" She responded, "Why don't you know? You are the leader?" What went through my mind was: *Why don't I know? Why don't I know what your child's grades were last school year? I wasn't even here. Why don't YOU know? You mean, you went the entire summer and didn't inquire to see if he was promoted or retained? When I asked who his teacher was (thinking I could have them speak with you), you said, "You didn't know."* However, after I calmed those thoughts, what finally came out of my mouth was, "Mom, again, my apologies. If you can provide me with a current number, I will have the counselor contact you. She said, "Why do you need my number? You are the principal. You should have it." She walked off. I then clicked my heels, opened my eyes, and realized, "Dorothy, you are not in Kansas anymore."

We live. We learn. We lead.

There are some things you will not know as you embark upon your journey and learn the power of your voice and elevate. I thought I was ready when I started day one. I decreed and declared, "My experiences have prepared me for every obstacle and every hindrance that may come against me." I shouted, "I was born to win. This is what I have prepared for my entire life!" "My footsteps are ordered. I always win!" However, after exposure, experience takes another meaning. I still have the same leadership declarations I speak over myself today. Although the challenges of being a leader vary, my faith in Him who has called, equipped, and anointed me has not.

There is always a first. For example, I never had an employee engage in a verbal altercation with another staff member in front of parents. I never had two employees engage in a physical confrontation at work. I never had an employee accuse me of saying something that I did not say. I never had someone call in sick and then post a video of themself at the airport boarding a flight on social media and say, "It wasn't me." I never had an employee walk around and openly sow discord and strife among the staff. When those things happened, I didn't know how to react during those instances because I didn't have any prior knowledge in those areas. As a leader, I am sure you have a personal list of "I never had…" moments.

Through them all, we learn to win. I said **learn**. It doesn't mean that you won't have to fight and press your way through. I learned to follow policy and protocol, not my opinion. If you don't have your list, I can hear my grandmother, Alice Thomas, say, "Just keep living. You will."

Chapter Seven

We all Need Time to Grow

The Spirit of Familiarity

There is that quick millisecond when you have to decide as a leader to fight or flight or to speak or remain silent realizing that each choice presents a set of unique circumstances. There is always a cost. Which can you live with? When do you push forward? When do you fall back? Not every comment deserves a response. Dr. Myles Munroe shared, "We should never apply a permanent solution to a temporary problem. If we are not careful, we will make a decision out of pressure, and not purpose." Learn to follow your inside voice. One of my favorite sayings is, "Silence may be misunderstood, but it cannot be misquoted." I am not saying you always will have time to pause and think of an answer in every situation that presents itself. What I am saying is that as we grow in leadership, we learn the importance of staffing those around us who have the strengths, experiences, and talents that we don't have. Some challenges may not allow you the courtesy of saying, "Let me get back with you tomorrow."

We have to be good in the skin that we are in and reach out to a team member or colleague for guidance. Otherwise, you will find yourself surrounded with people who act and sound like you, but they don't have the same spirit as you. *Why did they do that?* That's what you hired. *Why did they say that?* That's who they are. You thought it would be good to be the smartest person in the room - Mr. or Mrs. Know it All. Therefore, you hired people who always would have to come to you to get an answer. You think it makes you important. What it does is make you tired. How many of you realize that people come in seasons in your life? I am thankful for the people with whom I was surrounded ten years ago. If they entered my life today, the lessons I learned may be different unless I am the same person I was then and didn't learn the lesson the first time. Hopefully, I learned from them, and I trust they learned from me. If our paths crossed today, they would not be the "gap filler" I needed yesterday. As you mature, you should be able to look back and say, "I enjoyed that period in my life, but the time came for me to move on. The well dried up. I no longer can get the sustenance I need. I am not that person or that leader anymore." Learn to let people go and move on. If not, you may find that which satisfied your thirst for leadership yesterday is what dehydrates you today.

We all have our partners, our faithful few, or our ride or die crew. We have those people who know exactly what to say to get us back on our feet. What happens when *that* which was used to be a floater for you or a life saver now has become an anchor? What happens when *that* connection or *that* relationship which used to undergird and support you is now weighing you down? What happens when you realize the one who needs to change his/her circle is you? What happens when you have said too much? What happens when the spirit of familiarity rears its ugly head? They are comfortable around you now. They know more than they should know about you and your personal affairs. You have allowed the line between employee and supervisor to become smeared, and now your ability to see clearly and lead fairly has become compromised. You can't lead like you need to lead them because they know too much about you.

Learn the art of silence.

Keep your business to yourself and keep your mouth closed.

It

I shared with a group of leaders that exposure is an integral part of experience. Once you have been exposed to "it," you can have a better perspective on how to handle "it" when "it" appears again. Additionally, I can assure you that "it" will. It may not look the same, smell the same, or respond in the same way. However, trust me. "It" is, and "it" is waiting on the leader inside you to rise to the occasion. Who do you have around you who may have a victory conquering the "it" that has taken you out in times past?

We have to be able to discern between those who are in our corner and those who are in our circle. Know when to go to each one based on the situation or when the "it" has been presented. We can't haphazardly make decisions without considering the consequences that will come from them. I still vividly remember Sr. Pastor Emeritus Allen McNair saying, "Sam, as a leader, you don't have a right to change company policy. You were hired to enforce it." He made the statement to me because I decided out of sympathy to help an employee, only to find out the employee had miscommunicated the truth regarding the matter. At the end, he said, "People will not always be honest with you. Just make sure that you are honest and fair with them. Leaders make decisions based on policy, not practice. That way, when it comes back, your boss will be able to support you."

As leaders, we can't always dismiss prior instances with our staff when a similar one emerges. We also can't assume that staff members are guilty of the offense this time. Be fair. Look at each encounter based on its own merit. Truth needs no defense. I remember sharing with a staff member, "If you tell me something, I will believe you and trust you until you give me a reason not to feel that way." Trust has different layers. This initial trust is just that - initial. Remember the times when you needed grace and it was given to you? Don't forget that when the time comes and that same grace needs to be extended to someone else. People should not be held captive to their last decision. We must give our up and coming leaders time to grow, time to learn the lesson, and time to help them develop from there. What if we pulled back your door #3? What would we find lurking there? As my grandmother used to say, "God don't like ugly, and He ain't too crazy about pretty. Do right by folks, and right will follow you."

The Pressure of a Moment:

Have you sent an email or made a comment and immediately wished you could've taken it back? It was sent, or it came from a mindset, a set of influences, that were more personal than professional. If it was any other time, your reply would have been different. Whether it was because you hadn't had your cup of coffee, you and your spouse had a disagreement before you left for work, your savings and your checking accounts were not lining up, or your child was acting like a younger version of you, and you didn't like what you saw. Or you had a meeting with your boss later that day, and you felt unprepared, you had a lot on your mind. At that moment, your mind and thoughts were overwhelmed with so many other conflicting priorities that you allowed those situations to frame your response. Moreover, it did not come out well. Experience teaches us that it is best to gauge where OUR mind is and what is driving our thoughts before we respond or react.

Should I wait before I have this conversation or send that email?

Have I made sure that my intentions are pure?

Have I looked at all of the data and potential causes of what may explain the behavior or action I am about to address? Am I allowing past experiences to cloud my judgment?

Is the employee facing a personal crisis that may be impacting his/her ability to perform his/her job? Have I even asked? Have I even spoken to the employee recently?

Have I had a conversation with the employee's supervisor who addressed the concern with me before I met him/her? Has the supervisor laid out a plan of support for the employee and provided feedback? Am I just "jumping and responding" based on what the supervisor told me because he/she was mad?

When it comes to being a leader, always remember that who you are on the inside always will speak more loudly than who you are on the outside. The personal set of core values in which you operate - fairness, honesty, integrity, positivity, and treating others the way we want to be treated - all influence and frame your way of thinking. In the end, those qualities will be apparent in your actions. The negative seeds that have been planted in your life over the years, if untended or not plucked up, will grow up, mature, and show up in your character. As you grow in grace and authority, take time to pause and work on yourself. Ask yourself, *If I sow this thought, deed, or action, will I reap the harvest I desire?*

Success is Predictable

Dr. Myles Munroe said, "Success is predictable, and so is failure." In other words, there are some steps that you and I can take that will increase our voice and expand our territory markedly. There are similar actions or steps that you and I can take as a leader that will reduce or diminish our voice. We all have something to say. The question we have to ask ourselves is, *Is anyone listening to what I am saying?* One of my favorite sayings by motivational speaker, Les Brown, is, "You gotta be hungry!" I often wondered why I heard it in almost (well, not almost) every speech he presented? It reminded me of one of my favorite scriptures from Romans 10:17 that says, "Faith (for any subject) comes by hearing and hearing (on that subject)." As I continue to grow personally and professionally, each time I listen to one of Les Brown's messages, and he uses that phrase, I realize I am not the same person who heard it last year, six months ago, or even yesterday. As a leader, situations come and go. We learn or grow from each encounter that we face. We learn how to accept the choices from the decisions we make and admit when the spirit of pride or arrogance prevailed when we should have humbled ourselves and exercised self-patience.

I had to forgive myself for those times when I was more concerned about pleasing others rather than doing what was right. I had to forgive myself for rushing into an action and not having another pair of shoes in my toolkit. The wingtips I wore to work were not the ones I needed when it rained that afternoon. The rain boots were not designed to give me the support I needed when I had to chase after a student to prevent him from running out the front door. It was the experience that taught me the value of knowing which pair worked best in that situation. Thank God for His grace when I had to make decisions only with the single pair of shoes I wore. I am not my last mistake, and neither are you.

If we are not careful, the spirit of comparison will cause us to, as Robert McDonald said, "Doubt in the darkness what God has spoken to us in the light." Leadership evolves, and we do too. The only person I am competing against is me. *Am I better today than I was yesterday?* That is the only question we should ask ourselves. We shouldn't ask ourselves, *Am I better than the leader in the office next door? Is my business or company making as much money as his/her company? Are my children doing as well as my sister's children? They just bought a new car. I have to upgrade mine, or she will think that I am not doing as well as she is doing.* If we are not rooted and grounded in who we are, we will find ourselves trying to live someone else's dream.

You do you. Your success, your next level, and your destiny is tied to your authenticity. Dr. Myles Munroe said, "Leadership is personal. Then, it becomes corporate. You have to work on you." I remember reading a quote by Neil deGrasse Tyson that said, "It is a problem when you know enough about a subject to think you are right but not enough to know you are wrong." We all need time to grow. Joel Osteen said, "Without Goliath, you won't take your throne. Without Judas, you won't reach your destiny. Without the naysayers, you won't become all you were created to be." In other words, it is our victories that prepare us for our next encounter.

Chapter Eight

The Leader Makes the Difference

I read an article that spoke about understanding what is required before you assume the mantle of leadership. The author shared that the mantle of leadership remains with the position and not the person. Yes, leaders must be talented and qualified to serve, and they must possess the competencies necessary to be effective. However, when a person leaves a leadership role at one level and transitions into another role, the mantle falls to the NEXT person if he/she chooses to accept it. It is not automatic. When you are elevated or promoted, you need to take on the mantle designed for your NEW status. The one you don't want to release from your last role might not have the grace to sustain you in the role where you are headed now.

Recently, I watched a documentary on a recent shuttle launch. The commentator shared how each step in the process provides the foundation for successful completion of the next phase. I found it interesting that after the rocket boosters fall from the shuttle, the shuttle continues its ascent into space. The boosters achieved their purpose, and when it was time for them to fall off, they did what they were created to do. They fell. What boosters (relationships, practices, unforgiveness) are you holding on to that you should have released years ago? You have reached your initial ascent into leadership, yet you are hovering and asking yourself, *Why haven't I gone any higher?* We limit our ability to be effective because we try to take people with us when their purpose or season in our lives has ended. We need to release them, so that they can be repurposed to operate in the grace that comes with the role they will play for the next leader in waiting. Don't allow how you think, how you speak, and how you act to limit your elevation.

Shortly after I moved to Atlanta, a friend of my parents blessed me with some shoes he had purchased and rarely worn as well as some shoes that were gently used. As I tried on one particular pair, I noticed how comfortable they were. It seems as if they were tailor-made just for me. I was thankful that he released the "boosters" I needed, so they could serve a renewed purpose in my life. Just because the shoes were slightly worn, did not mean their worth had devalued. What are you refusing to accept from someone because it is not coming from a source that you think is worthy? Bishop T. D. Jakes said, "Some people may not have your faith, but they have your blessing. Treat people right. You never know who God is going to use to bless you."

John Maxwell's *Law of the Inner Circle* shares with us that every leader's potential is determined by the people closest to him/her. If the people are strong, then the leader can make a huge impact. If the people are weak, the leader cannot. No matter how good you think your people are, if they are not strong leaders, they will hinder your ability to take your organization or business where it needs to go. The law of the inner circle states that when the inner circle – those closest to the leader – goes to a new level so does the organization. Our goal as leaders is to prepare others for their next level by creating a relationship of mutual respect and honor, so the leader's ceiling becomes the follower's floor. If you look around, and you are no higher than you were before elevation, check your inner circle. They may be the reason for your decline. Bishop William Murphy expressed it this way, "Part of the problem we face as leaders is that we are surrounded by people who can't help us. You are limiting the future of your organization by the circle you keep." There is a proverb that says, "If you lie down with dogs, you will get up with fleas." In other words, we should watch the company we keep. How long will you continue to scratch before you realize that you have been impacted by what you are around?

I once heard a minister at a funeral say, "We are born. We live our lives. Then, we die." I thought, *Well, that is a direct way to look at it.* However, as I rode home that afternoon, I started to reflect on what he shared and my impact on those I encounter on a daily basis. What I gathered was this. We are born. We live our lives. We die. Yep, that was it. The heart of the message was that those of us who still have an opportunity to make a difference should look at how we live and make sure that the potentially 10,000 people we will influence over the course of our lives experience a life that's better because we were in it. On behalf of all the aspiring leaders who are looking for the "right" influences to come across their path, you don't have to be perfect. In my opinion, you just have to be good enough. That's all. Better today than yesterday. A forest fire can be started by a single spark. Make the decision to be an igniter for someone that you meet along the way. Even if you have to do it alone.

Lessons Learned Along the Way

Stop trying to carry a load that your life and call to leadership were not designed to handle.

Stop trying to imitate what someone else is doing. Stay in your lane.

Stop allowing people to hold you in bondage to the leader who was there before you. Know your worth.

Stop looking in the mirror and seeing who you used to be.

Stop living in the result of a choice you made. Sometimes, you win. Sometimes, you learn. Know the difference and move on.

Stop settling for the status quo such as the "we have always done it this way here" or the "that is just the way it is." As a leader, I am not a thermostat. I am a thermometer. It is up to me to SET the temperature, culture, and climate in my environment. I do not RESPOND to it.

Stop before you move. Are you ready or are you anxious? You do not want to be the leader who steps out, only to find that you do not have the faithfulness to stick it out.

Stop and look at your fruit. What does it say about you?

The motivation to share my experiences from my journey to leadership and notes from my journal over the years isn't to imply that I am an expert on the subject. It is not to persuade you to lead the way I do or say that I always have made the best decisions because I have not. I will be the first to admit that I do not have all the answers. No leader does. What worked for me Monday that made me confident did not solve the challenges that Tuesday presented. If nothing else, the pandemic has taught us that we no longer can lead the way we used to lead. Our idea of normal is skewed based on prior experiences that we have undergone and the constant potential of another unknown.

The purpose for me writing this book is not to get you to think the way I think. My thinking is framed based on my experiences, exposure, and expectations. I can be the first to admit that some of them were flawed. However, I also can say that I learned from each encounter. The goal of me sharing my journey is to offer various perspectives about why people lead the way they do, share some of my failures and successes, and confirm what you already know.

You are enough.

Plant the seed for the future you desire. Work with others but place your faith and confidence in what God has shown you. Ask and believe that He will surround you with those who are critical to your success. Don't let a "no" stop your pursuit. Les Brown said, "Sometimes, we have to fail our way to success. If something is worth doing, it is worth doing wrong." Find out what does and does not work for you. Make the adjustment and keep going!

When one door closes, continue to knock. Another will open. I have to believe that. Psalm 23:3 KJV says, "He restoreth my soul: he leadeth me in paths of righteousness for his name's sake." For HIS name's sake. He wants it right with us, so He can be glorified! He always wins. If you want success, get on the winning team.

We each have prior experiences that led to positive changes in our character and our behavior. For me, it was the experience as a young man walking through an amusement park with a blister on the back of my foot. For my daughter, it was a trip of a lifetime scarred by discomfort because she wore shoes that she had not tried on beforehand. For you, it may be something completely different. Whatever path in which life takes you on your leadership journey, always remember that if a lesson is not learned, it will find a way to repeat itself. It is up to you to look in your Felix the Cat bag of tricks and pull out a pair of shoes that have been predestined for that assignment. Take them out, put them on, and lace them up. You are the leader. Your destiny awaits.

Meet Samuel Wayne West

Motivational Speaker, Educator, Leadership Coach, and Pastor

Samuel Wayne West is a sought-after motivational speaker and educator. He worked in full-time ministry in a variety of roles, including Daycare Director, Principal (K-8 Academy), Pastoral Coach/Trainer, Assistant Pastor, and Senior Associate Pastor before entering the academic arena. During his twenty-plus years as an educator, he has served as an administrator at the pre-school, elementary, middle, and high school levels across private, charter, and public school settings.

He currently serves as a school administrator and principal coach for a school district in the metro Atlanta area. West was a 2010 – 2011 district finalist for teacher of the year, named principal of the year for the 2017-2018 school year and was again named a district finalist for principal of the year for the 2018-2019 school year.

As the founder of Qwest Consulting, LLC, West believes that the ability to envision and articulate clearly what you see on the inside of you has always been a critical component of successful leadership. An ordained minister and motivational speaker, West shares practical tips and strategies that will propel your vision forward. His style of ministry (edutainment) delivers a message that educates, entertains, and integrates real life application with theory through his 'What Sam Said' series. *A Promise Kept* is his first book.

West was born in Montezuma, Georgia, and graduated from Peach County High School. He received his undergraduate degree from Fort Valley State University. West earned his master's degree in Educational Management from Strayer University, his Educational Specialist degree from Liberty University, and his leadership certification from Georgia State University. He is the son of two retired educators, Clyde and Bettye Zachery, and the brother of Nikki Zachery Cooper. He lives in metro Atlanta with his wife, Katriece, and their daughter, Samaria.